A

WOMAN'$

WORTH:

7 KEY ESSENTIALS TO FINANCIAL INDEPENDENCE

By

Reshell Smith, MBA, CFP®

Copyright © 2018 Reshell Smith, MBA, CFP®

ISBN-13: 978-1724464040

ISBN-10: 1724464043

Published by:

Reshell Smith, MBA, CFP®

Edited by:

Dr. Ruth L. Baskerville

www.ruthbaskerville.com

INTRODUCTION

As a woman and a professional in the workplace, I've seen too often that we lack the understanding to take control of our finances. We barely understand the need to analyze every aspect of our spending. We need to change our mindset from just living and spending to living, spending, giving and investing. It's a concept many women have not been exposed to growing up, and a concept that eluded me during my formative years, as well.

Now I'm in a position to share what I know will bring women the control, the confidence, and the skill set to "handle your business," as they say. I wrote this book to bless readers with seven concrete steps towards becoming financially independent. Perhaps you've never thought about it, or thought about how you could achieve it. Well, look no further!

Are you ready to *finally* take control of your finances and live the life you were born to live? If you said, *"Yes,"* then you are in the right place. This book will provide you with the seven key essential pieces of information that you need to start your journey towards financial independence.

It will:

Educate you on important money issues;

Empower you to make smarter money decisions;

Inspire you to take responsibility for your financial future.

I have had the pleasure of working in the financial industry for over twenty years, during which time I've worked with many people of different ages, ethnicities and socioeconomic backgrounds. They have had different educational and financial backgrounds, too, and all of this presented me with the exciting challenge of figuring out how best to meet each of their financial needs.

By far, the greatest benefits for me were gaining my clients' trust, and building a strong rapport that caused us to bond on some level. In our initial conversation, I learned about their families, their jobs, their hobbies and most importantly, how they manage their money. Because they were willing to make changes to their lives, particularly their spending habits, I was able to help them navigate through their financial puzzles and make their financial dreams become a reality. What a rewarding experience that was....and still is today!

But I quickly realized that I was serving the needs of only those persons who sought me out. I had not even conceived of an outreach program that would bring me before larger groups of women who likely didn't know what they didn't know about finances. If you don't think or know you have a problem, how can you fix it?

So while I was elated to have the positive experiences with my clients, I always felt like I could do more. More often than not, I felt like there was that *one thing* missing. Actually, it was that *one person* who was missing—THE WOMAN. I DIDN'T GET THE OPPORTUNITY TO WORK WITH ENOUGH WOMEN. Don't get me wrong, I had nothing against men--I just have a personal passion for helping smart women to be come savvy finance managers.

I knew it then and I know it now that my passion is to educate and help women become financially literate. I wanted to share my knowledge with women and give them the power to stand on their own two feet. The time has come for women to shake things up and become MAVERICKS! This book will get you started on the journey to do just that. I created it to provide women (...and smart men) with **seven** key essentials that can be used in life and in business.

Reshell Smith, MBA, CFP®

Table of Contents

Essential 1
Every Woman Should Know Her Money Attitude

Women are so important to the economy, especially the American economy. I say this because they are increasingly becoming more educated and making major moves in the workforce. Over the past two decades, women's portion of household income has steadily increased. As a matter of fact, in more and more households, the woman is considered the breadwinner. This should give women cause to be pleased with our collective progress in what used to be a male-dominated field.

However, as many of us already know because we are doing the same or similar work to men in some fields, women still make a lesser salary than men, and may even receive fewer benefits. This is troubling because women have steadily gotten more education with advanced degrees. They may bring more experience to a position as well, and yet women still make less than men—go figure! We've got some work to do, ladies!

Now many of us have heard everything I've said so far. But did you know that women earn on average about 77-79 cents for every dollar a man makes? True, that gap used to be significantly wider because employers assumed that their male employees needed more money because they were the breadwinners. Times changed and more women went to work, but the attitude of employers, particularly men who dominated the top management positions, remained the same.

Well, men's minds and attitudes may be archaic, but women need to know our worth. With statistics showing an increasing impact of women on the economy, it's important for women to understand our *"money attitude."* Knowing how you *feel* about money and what it *means* to you is key. By this I mean the reason why you spend too much, or why you are in debt, or why you make impulsive decisions, or even why you hoard money – all of this is your "money attitude." Your feelings about money will have a direct impact on how you make money decisions.

For example, I recall a time when I would get very large bonuses at my job. Because I loved flashy things and I was being very materialistic, instead of investing those bonuses I spent them all. The consequence was that now, I don't have that money invested for my retirement, and those shiny objects are no longer shiny. I realize now I have to work longer than I would have, if I had invested earlier in my career.

On the other hand, once I saw the big picture in terms of my financial future, I remember receiving a large income tax refund. I no longer desired to purchase shiny, expensive items. Instead, I used much of it to pay down my debt, and still had some to put away for savings. That was a smart move in two ways, because my total debt was reduced, and my emergency fund was solvent.

I have witnessed many women who are making a great salary, but who make some unfortunate "big money" mistakes. Most of those mistakes were made because they were not aware of their money attitude. They made purchase after purchase. They gave money to family members without requiring them to pay it back. They made investments without doing necessary research, and those investments failed. Some of these women learned by bringing on a professional like me, who helped them create a financial plan. Others are still making the same mistakes, and I can see their retirement and emergency funds slipping away with each year.

You can avoid making these mistakes by knowing your own money attitude. Are you a *Saver* or *Spender*? Are you a *Planner* or *Dodger*? Do you consider yourself to be *Rational* or *Impulsive*? Would others describe you as a *Show-off* or *Grower?* If you are a saver, more than likely, you are setting aside a certain amount of your monthly income for retirement or emergencies, or perhaps for a major purchase like a home. If you are a spender, you spend, spend, spend, without regard for the critical importance of saving. Spenders more than likely are spending what they bring in, and saving what might be left over like crumbs on a plate.

Planners are people who more than likely have the professional help to create a realistic financial plan so they can reach a future goal. They don't mind delayed gratification. At the same time, dodgers are people who totally avoid any type of financial plan. They generally do not have future goals written out. It's like they have ideas in their mind for the future, but they have no idea how to reach their professed goals. This chaos spills into every part of their lives, which is problematic.

When we think of the word "rational," we think someone is using reason and logic to make decisions. A rational spender would naturally save first, and save the most from whatever income the person has. But, an impulsive spender acts in haste, without forethought. It's a behavior that can be changed, but much like the alcoholic, they must first recognize that they have a problem, and earnestly seek professional help.

Finally, do you consider yourself, as described by others, to be a showoff? It's pretty obvious what a showoff is in every aspect of life. In finances, a showoff throws money around, impulsively treats groups of people to food and drink, and shows off big jewelry, clothing, cars, and homes. They make sure everyone around them knows they "have it all." Well, what they have all of are the bills for those extravagant demonstrations of wealth and power!

The opposite of a showoff is a grower. Growers may have a lot of money, but they are looking for ways to increase their money. They buy real estate so they can flip houses and get more real estate. They invest wisely in the stock market and make their money grow. We say of these people that they "make money while they sleep." These are the people who understand the value of money. Money should produce wealth for the next generation and beyond. Proverbs 13:22 says, *"A good man leaves an inheritance to his children's children...."*

Maybe you are a combination of two or three of these. Knowing your money attitude is important because, if you are the breadwinner, you will probably have significant input when it comes to making financial decisions. You will really need to sit down and think about how you will handle your family's finances when things like emergencies arise. Will you be OK going into debt or will you have an emergency fund already set up that you can tap into when something unexpected arises?

Quick Tip: For your emergency fund, starting out, you want to set aside as quickly as possible at least $1,000.00. That amount can cover the average emergency in the family, on the job, or anywhere else in your life. However, you want to work your way up to three-to-six months of living expenses set aside, in case you either lose your job, or experience something catastrophic that causes you to need a large sum of money quickly. You should save this money in an account that you can access easily, but not as easily as putting it under your mattress.

I'd like to take this a step further and ask that you reflect on your childhood and teenage years. Think about your parents' actions when they had to make hard money decisions. A lot of your money attitude is based on your upbringing. For example, if you grew up less fortunate, meaning you were without a lot of material things, you may be more inclined to splurge on things your parents were never able to afford to give you. Depending on social and peer pressures you faced during your school years, you may have told yourself you would never be in lack when you grew up. Making lavish purchases comforts your inner self and makes you feel that you have made good on that promise.

Never mind what happens when the bills for those elaborate spending purchases comes due.

A different attitude would be, since you know what it feels like to be less fortunate in terms of material possessions, you may be adamant about not being in that position again. Therefore, you may be more inclined to save and be frugal. You could take that to the extreme, just like the person who spends without self-control. You would raise children to appear to be less fortunate, when you had the funds to give them more than you had growing up.

Not only that, but you would deny yourself, just as you were denied as a child, and probably be miserable when you finally realized that your whole life was one of sacrifice and denial, with little pleasure. There's an expression that says, *"You can't take it with you, and you can't send it ahead."* All of us deserve to enjoy some of the fruits of our labor while we're on this earth.

Another great example of when knowing your money attitude may be helpful is the infamous "stroll through the mall." What will you do when you see the big red sale sign hanging over a great pair of shoes? If you are impulsive, you will probably buy them just because they are on sale. If you are rational, you will likely love them, but leave those babies right where they are. If you're a showoff, not only will you buy a pair of shoes for you, but you will also buy a pair in every color available, or buy a pair for someone else. A showoff has to be in a position to tell someone what he or she did for him. A showoff craves the recognition for having abundance. As you learn more about your money attitude, you may find that how you handle money depends on the importance or urgency of the situation.

©Istockphoto.com/keeweeboy

As you get a better understanding of your money attitude, consider different ways of improving that attitude. Here are a few helpful habits I suggest you start to practice:

- Try to speak about money using positive language, such as, *"I am increasing my net worth"* or *"I am a money magnet"*
- Place your money neatly in your wallet, so that you always know the amount you have.
- Save loose change in a piggy bank, and at the end of the year, use it to pay down debt.
- Keep track of where every dollar goes. Create money buckets or use envelopes. Label each envelope with an expense item and put cash in the envelope to cover the expense. When it's gone, it's gone!
- Keep track of ALL your income, not just salary. Keep track of dividends, refunds, rebates, online sales, etc.
- Have an attitude of gratitude. When you receive unexpected discounts or unexpected checks, be grateful!

Essential 2
Every Woman Should Know Her Net Worth

By now, I hope I've given you much to think about in determining your "money attitude." I'll bet you never associated "money" with "attitude" before, but they definitely belong together! So what is "net worth"? We know that our net pay is what we actually receive, after taxes from our gross earnings. But every woman should know her net worth. How much are YOU really worth?

In layman's terms, if you sell all that you own and pay off all that you owe, what you have left is your net worth. There are only two outcomes to this kind of math. You will either have a positive net worth or a negative net worth. A positive net worth says that you own more than you owe. Older people may have called that a "nest egg," or "retirement security," but it meant that they had saved wisely over many years, and they must have spent wisely too!

For nearly all women, this is where you want to be. This is the financial position that you want to be in. As you go through the cycles of life, a positive net worth is what you want to strive for. When we're young, we think we'll live forever, and we think we have plenty of time to save. We may feel we owe it to ourselves to enjoy life while we're young. And we interpret that word "enjoy" to mean we must spend money as fast as we make or receive it.

However, as we go through those cycles of life I mentioned above, we realize all too quickly that the expression "saving for a rainy day" has meaning. When we spend all we have, we have nothing in reserve, and we put ourselves in positions of having to be borrowers. Had we observed the principles in my first chapter, we would be lenders and not borrowers.

Despite the faulty thinking of youth, most of us want to steadily increase our positive net worth. To increase your net worth, consider these seven strategies:

The first is to always pay yourself first! For example, when you get paid from work, the first person who should get a portion of your pay is you. You put a certain percentage of your pay in your retirement, your emergency fund or savings. Most experts would suggest saving 10% – 15% of your paycheck. If you take that away off the top, you will be able to pay yourself. The rule of thumb is to "save before you spend," not "save what's left after you've spent."

The second strategy is to save as much as you can, as often as you can. Every time you get paid, or you receive a bonus or commission, or when you get income from a part-time job, you should save something. I tell my clients, "When you get a raise, save your raise or a portion of your raise." You lived successfully before you got the raise, so if you are wise, you will discipline yourself to live without all or some of it now that you have a raise. Let me be more specific. If you get a 4% raise on your existing salary, you should either save the entire 4% increase, or you should consider saving 2% of it and spending the other 2%.

Here's a third strategy. Look for opportunities to grow your money -- like investing in the stock market. When I say for you to look for opportunities to grow your money, I mean that, instead of leaving money in cash or in a savings account, consider investing in the stock market. Keeping cash under a mattress gets you no extra return. And if you put your cash into a bank savings account, your interest is minimal. However, by investing in the stock market, you are allowing your money to make money by investing in companies that have opportunity to grow.

The fourth strategy is one that we've heard all our lives. *"Debt free is the way to be."* Maybe not our parents, but certainly financial experts would agree that we should strive to pay down our debts. Turn up the heat and be as aggressive as you can be when tackling your debts. You can double up on payments of some or all of your credit cards. Also, you can pay off the credit card with the smallest balance. Another idea is for you to pay off the credit card with the highest interest rate. Doing any of these is guaranteed to reduce your debt.

If you own a home, renegotiate loans and/or refinance your mortgage so that you can lock in a lower interest rate and pay more towards the principal. This strategy will shave years off your mortgage. Too often, we secure the typical 30-year mortgage at a certain rate of interest, and we never think about it again. However, I'm suggesting you pay attention to the current mortgage rate, and if it is lower than what you agreed to pay when you purchased your mortgage, it may be smart to renegotiate the loan and get the lower interest rate. Be careful of hidden fees, but if it makes financial sense, go ahead and do it.

The sixth strategy would be to reduce your expenses. Start by cutting back on your discretionary spending. These are things you buy that you could really live without (i.e. dining out, concerts, movies, excessive shopping). Have you ever added up the cost of buying your morning coffee and a breakfast sandwich on the way to work? The cost, multiplied by the week, the month and the year, will likely produce a figure that would be staggering to anyone. You need to add up the purchases you make regularly, that seem so insignificant at the time. Once you do that, it should be easy to cut back on these expenses. "Bye, bye $5.00 coffee!"

Let's say you've done some of everything I've suggested in the first six strategies to get control of your finances. If you have the time and the skills, consider taking on a part-time job to bring in extra income. Instead of coming home from your job and planting yourself in front of the television, you could go to a part-time job and realize real cash by the end of the time you would spend watching a movie or being on social media. Today, with the Internet bringing us in contact with millions of people in minutes, you could start a home-based business. This could end up being very lucrative, and if you've got the time and talent, you should try to get the treasure too.

If you incorporate even some of these things into your daily living, you will start to see changes in your net worth. Don't be surprised if you see changes occurring frequently, especially if you have investments where the risks are small, but the potential return is good. By the way, I suggest you never attempt to navigate through the stock market without a financial advisor to guide you. You don't want to, as they say, lose the "shirt off your back." That means you have either invested more than you could bear to lose, or invested without doing the research to choose stocks wisely. Get help to make wise decisions because the stock market is "unforgiving," although when approached correctly, it will surely increase your net worth.

Investing in the stock market will cause fluctuations in your net worth. It's logical that when the market shifts, it affects your net worth. If you take your money out of the stock market or other personal investments designed to help you save money long-term, you may discover that your net worth is negative, which means you probably have some work to do. Unfortunately, you are not alone. According to experts, about one in every five U.S. households owe more than they own. You will see that, as you start to incorporate the things I mentioned earlier, your negative net worth will start to shift and eventually turn positive. This is not something that will happen overnight. For many, it may take several years. That includes me as well. I did not always take my advice, but I am following it now!

Knowing whether your net worth is positive or negative is important because it lets you know the state of your financial health. However, it's probably not something that you should check daily because you will have fluctuations every day. If you are working with a professional like me, he/she may analyze your net worth at the end of each year to make sure you are on track to reach your goals.

Essential 3
Every Woman Should Know Her Credit Score

Why is it important for you to know your credit score? Although you may not like it, your credit score is how you are judged by others financially. I know that it doesn't tell your whole financial story, but lenders see it as an indicator of how you have managed your debts historically. In a nutshell, it's all about how you handle *debt*. DEBT...not assets, not income...just DEBT.

So, for example, if you have $1 million dollars in a savings account, it is not reflected on your credit report. Credit scores represent the way you have historically managed your debt. They do not directly reflect your income or other sources of wealth. I know wealthy people who have unfavorable credit scores because they mismanage their debt.

Below is a pie chart that explains how your credit score is computed.

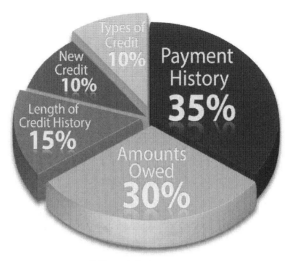

©NextAdvisor.com

Although the ultimate goal for all of us is to be debt-free, there may come a time when you need to take on a loan, apply for a credit card or apply for a new job. In instances like these, you want to have a strong credit score. Some employers, especially those in the financial industry, correctly feel that if you cannot manage your own debt, you are not in a position to manage the finances of others. When you have not demonstrated good decision-making in terms of your finances, it impacts employers' perceptions of your credibility in the workplace. You may not get the job.

As you can see on the chart below, a strong or very good credit score is 720 and above. When your score gets to 720, lenders start to consider you very low risk. Being what they call "very low risk" means creditors feel confident giving you money or real property because they believe that you have a high probability of repaying the money. This is one of the ways "the rich get richer and the poor get poorer." When you have no financial struggles, you pay all your bills on time and earn excellent credit scores. That, in turn, gives lenders confidence in doing business with you at the most attractive interest rates you command. They will likely offer you more favorable terms on a loan. Thus, you pay your loan off quicker, having spent less of your money on the interest for that loan. The rich get richer!

On the other hand, when you have money issues, particularly if you're living from paycheck to paycheck, you are likely to fall behind in bills and credit card payments. Even if this happens infrequently, it could take up to seven years to have negative marks removed from your credit report. How about if you never miss a payment, but need to make partial payments? Did you know that, even if your creditor allows a portion of the monthly bill to come in after the official due date, it could have a negative effect on your credit score if the payment is more than thirty days delinquent?

When the person with the poor credit score goes to make a large purchase, the lender could impose the highest interest rate because the borrower is considered "high risk" for paying back the loan. Higher interest rates mean it will take you significantly longer to finish paying for your purchase. Refer to the chart below showing colors to match credit scores from very poor to excellent. We all want to get to that target score, which means you need to be disciplined and strategic. Make the following practices a habit:

Pay your bills on time every month. In general, you don't want to be more than thirty days late. This will positively affect your credit score. Also, pay off your credit card balances in full every month. By doing so, you are avoiding paying interest and potential late fees.

I'll bet you never heard that, despite the spending limit on a credit card, you should never let your balance be more than 30% of the limit for the credit card. This positively affects your credit utilization ratio, which is the amount you have borrowed, compared to your credit limit.

Do not apply for a lot of credit. If you have to take on a new loan, only take on a loan that you can afford. It's tempting to receive those credit cards in the mail that say, *"Just call to activate your credit limit of thousands of dollars."* The wording on the "pre approved" letters is flattering, but don't be fooled by that flattery because you will fall into the most common trap among debtors when you activate the card and begin spending. Without the discipline I mentioned in the chapters above, you may find yourself falling into those traps.

As often as you can, make sure you pay more than the minimum payment required each month. You end up paying the debt off faster, you pay less interest, and this has a positive effect on your overall credit score.

Additionally, do not close old accounts UNLESS you are charged an annual fee or you feel that you will be tempted to use the credit card. There are a couple of reasons why you do not want to do this. Say, you have a credit card for a long period of time, and your balance is zero. You still have access to the limit of that credit card, not to mention a good history with the credit card holder. Once you close that account, you may be negatively impacting your credit utilization ratio because, now your total credit amount available is less. Also, you lose the recording of the good history you had with the credit card you closed.

Make sure you have a good mix of credit (i.e. revolving credit, installment loan, mortgage and car payment). You don't want, for example, to have all your debt come from revolving credit at department stores. Diversity in the kinds and amounts of money you owe helps your credit score.

Make sure that you check for errors and omissions on your credit report. You want your credit report to be as accurate as possible. Make sure that your full name is correctly spelled and that all of the addresses listed are actually yours. Check to see that your payment history is accurately reflected. You may have a credit card where you've developed a good payment history, and it's not part of your report. That's an omission you want to correct immediately. These are just a few examples of errors or omissions. The important thing is that you are cognizant of what good credit scores are all about, and how they impact your life.

EXCELLENT	750 and ABOVE
VERY GOOD	720-749
FAIR to GOOD	660-719
POOR	551-659
BAD	550 and BELOW

When it comes to YOUR credit, you should know where you stand, especially if you are considering making a major purchase. Everyone is entitled to one free credit report per year from each of the main credit reporting agencies— Equifax, Experian and TransUnion. To obtain a copy of your free credit report online, visit www.annualcreditreport.com. To obtain a free credit score, go to www.creditkarma.com or www.creditsesame.com.

Tip: If you want to get free reports throughout the year, spread your requests out. For example, request a free report in January from Equifax, four months later request a free report from Experian, and four months later request a free report from TransUnion.

Essential 4
Every Woman Should Know Her Short-Term and Long-Term Money Goals

When you set a goal, you are attempting to reach a desired result. To reach that desired result, you have to devise a plan or strategy that will give you the best chance of being successful. That means you will have to work to achieve your goal. You can't just set a goal and *hope* you will accomplish it—you have to *do* something. You have to take action. I encourage my clients to set S.M.A.R.T goals. S.M.A.R.T is an acronym that stands for:

Specific (Be specific about your goals. They should be detailed and clear.)

Measurable (Apply a value to your goal, like a dollar amount or a time.)

Attainable (Your goals should be reasonable and you should have the necessary resources.)

Relevant (Your goals should link to your life or your business.)

Time-Bound (Your goals should have an end date that is achievable.)

©Istockphoto.com/marekuliasz

As I said above, it's important not to just have a goal, you need to have a smart goal. Below are two examples of contrasting goals, and I believe you will agree that the smart choice is the best choice.

Ineffective Goal: *"My goal this year is to save enough money to travel to Mexico."* This is an ineffective goal because it doesn't follow the S.M.A.R.T. Goal strategy. We don't know how much money is needed, nor the timeframe for saving the money needed. It's vague, and therefore likely not to be attained.

S.M.A.R.T. Goal: *"I want to save $1,000 by July 5th for my trip to Mexico. I will deposit $200 a month into my travel fund for the next 5 months."* This is not just throwing words into the air. It is specific, measurable, attainable, relevant and timely. Therefore, it's guaranteed to be accomplished, as long as you put the money in the travel fund according to the plan.

Incomplete Goal: *"I need to lose a few pounds before the summer so I can fit into my swimsuit."* No comment necessary!

S.M.A.R.T. Goal: *"I need to lose ten pounds by the end of May so I can fit into my swimsuit. I'm going to walk a mile a day with a target of losing two pounds per month for five months."* No comment necessary!

When you are setting goals, divide them into two broad categories: short-term and long-term. Short-term goals can usually be achieved in a year or less. Long-term goals, however, normally take longer than a year, with some taking many years. This is a "rule of thumb," based on what experts have said.

Common Short-Term Money Goals

Get organized and improve your debt management. This is a short-term goal that mainly requires you to change your behavior. Getting organized and managing your debt better may mean that you need to create spreadsheets to track your debt, or perhaps download a debt management app. This will help you see the debts that you have, and track your progress.

Also, create an achievable budget. A budget tells you what you can do, not what you can't do. Sometimes, people look at budgets, thinking that the budgets will constrain them. The opposite is true because that budget will show you how far your money can go. What's important is that you create a budget that represents your specific income and expenses, based on your lifestyle. Your budget should be used as a guide to help you maintain your current lifestyle, or, if necessary, change your lifestyle. If your budget shows that you have surplus income, you may consider options to save more. If your budget shows that you have a deficit, that is an opportunity to decide if you need to make more money or cut back on expenses.

Build an emergency fund. Experts say that we should have 3-6 months of living expenses saved for unexpected events. An unexpected event may include job loss, death in the family or a major car repair. Depending on your living expenses, it may be challenging to save 3-6 months of living expenses. If you can't put this lump sum aside, then a way to build on your emergency fund would be to establish a S.M.A.R.T. Goal. You would determine a specified time period, and divide the total amount you need by the number of months you have.

Pay down credit card debt. This actually can be a short-term or long-term goal, depending on how much you have to pay down. When you are paying down your credit card debt, you can either pay off the small balances first, or pay down the cards with the highest interest rate first. I like the idea of getting rid of those small pesky balances first. I believe it will help build momentum and give you a sense of accomplishment.

Start investing. Invest as much as you can, as often as you can. You can establish an investment account in a few minutes. It doesn't take a lot of time, nor does it take a lot of money. There are some great apps that you can set up in a matter of minutes and start investing immediately with as little as $5.00.

Hire a professional to help you with your finances. Handling your finances on your own can be challenging. Sometimes, you need guidance from a professional to help you navigate through the clutter of your finances. Oftentimes, professionals may have tools and resources that can help you achieve your financial goals. These are tools and resources you probably don't know about, but they are avenues for you to take advantage of.

Common Long-Term Money Goals

Save for retirement. *"I just want to be comfortable and enjoy my retirement,"* is the same line that I have been hearing for over twenty years! Saving for retirement is almost always on my clients' goal lists. This is because people are living longer, and today, retirement looks differently from the day when our grandparents reached retirement age. We are vibrant, wanting to travel and have new experiences for which we've worked all our lives. We need the financial means to realize our dreams.

Save for college. This is a common long-term goal for parents who want to set aside money over years to be sure their children have sufficient funds to go to college after high school. There are several ways to save for college, but the two most common ways to do this are a "pre-paid college plan" or a "529 savings plan." The "pre-paid college plan" basically means parents are pre-paying for the future costs of college today, while your children are growing. The "529 savings plan" allows you to save at your own pace for college, choosing your investment options.

Buy a home. It is still the "American Dream" to be a homeowner. Buying a home helps you build equity, and there is stability in living in the same place for a long time. There may be tax benefits at the end of the year, as well. There is security in home ownership, and you get to create long lasting family memories. The money goal is to have a down payment, and to be sure you have good credit, and, of course, to be able to furnish the new home. You want to be sure you can afford the payments and furnishings to create those special family memories.

Become Debt-Free. Depending on the size of your debt, this may be a long-term goal. For most people, the largest debt is the home mortgage, which can also be paid off sooner than the end date of the mortgage. One quick tip I use with my clients is that if they receive a tax refund, they make one extra payment on the principal of the loan. Done over time, this can shave off years of interest.

Increase your net worth. There is a formula for net worth, which mathematically is calculated to be your assets minus liabilities equals net worth. What that says is, if you were to liquidate everything you own and make it cash, and then you pay off everything you owe, what's left over is your net worth. There was a study done years ago showing that a single Black woman's net worth was $5.00, compared to a single white woman's worth of $42,600. Shocking!

Having said all of this, setting goals and consistently working on accomplishing them will give you the best opportunity to achieve financial independence (unless of course, you win the lottery—but that's a whole different story). Without goals, you may lack accountability and continue to make the same mistakes. Making the same mistakes over and over could cause you to miss out on opportunities to realize your dreams. SET your goals, BE S.M.A.R.T and BE accountable!

Tip: Partner with someone you trust and who has the same goals you do. You can encourage each other and track your progress together. It goes back to the importance of accountability. More important than having an exercise partner to hold us accountable for losing a few pounds, we need financial accountability because that impacts our lives today, and it affects our future as well.

Essential 5
Every Woman Should Know Her
Debt-Free Date

©Istockphoto.com/kmonroe2

Wouldn't you like to know when you can do your *"happy dance?"* I'm sure you would! However, you may have been in debt for so long that you have no earthly idea what it feels like to be debt-free. I believe that people have come to the conclusion that *"debt is ok, everybody has debt, so let's all do it."* I'm telling you today-- that it's not OK! Debt causes stress, it contributes to family fights, and it is one of the contributing factors to divorce. Many experts would say that it is the *MAIN* contributor to divorce. As a matter of fact, I read a study out of Kansas State University that found that couples get through issues of infidelity, raising and disciplining children, and dealing with relatives more easily than they can get over issues of money and finances. *"...there's a higher risk of divorce."*

You have to get out of this debt mess! It starts with changing your mindset. When you change the way you think about money, you can truly move to the next step--dealing with the numbers. For some, dealing with the numbers may be a matter of making a few tweaks in their budget. For others, it may be a bigger task that will take a longer period of time.

Here is what you need to do to become debt-free and financially independent:

1. Create an *effective* budget. An effective budget is one that requires you to live within

or below your means AND is achievable. If you create a budget that is too rigid to follow, you could be setting yourself up to be unsuccessful. For example, if you currently spend $600 per month on groceries and you create a budget that only allows you to spend $300 per month on groceries, you may be setting yourself up for failure. Perhaps you can eventually cut your grocery bill in half, but you need to gradually pull back.

2. Focus on changing your spending habits, especially the discretionary spending (i.e. eating out, entertainment, excessive clothing). You have to sacrifice and give up something if you truly want to be debt-free.

3. Write down a list of all of your debts. It doesn't matter how small or large they are, all debts should be included on the list.
   Tip: Review your credit report to make sure the debts that you owe are not obsolete.

4. Set specific goals for paying down your debts. Create a timetable that you can refer to and use as a guide. This will make you accountable.

5. Use the "snowball effect." That means that you pay down the small accounts first, and then you aggressively attack the larger accounts with the higher interest rates. By paying off those small accounts first, you will build momentum.

Tip: If you have credit cards, consider doing a balance transfer, but ONLY if it makes sense AND you are going to stick to the plan of paying off the debt before the promotional period ends.

6. Use cash more often, especially for daily essentials, so that you don't overspend. It's easy to keep swiping that credit card without realizing how fast your monthly bill increases. When you're out of cash, you're out of spending!

7. Get professional help! Hire a CERTIFIED FINANCIAL PLANNER™ professional. A planner may have tools and resources that you are not aware of. These tools and resources can help you reduce your debt quicker, increase your net worth, and cause you to do your happy dance sooner.

Although there are other things you can do to become debt-free, I have found these seven points to be the most effective. Following all of these together will ensure your ability to successfully reduce your debt until you reach the debt-free date you set as an attainable goal. But you have to work at it. You may occasionally go over your budget and spend more money than you have allotted for the week or the month. That is NOT a deal breaker! "Falling off the wagon a few times" should not destroy your plan and cause you to give up. Simply focus on the big picture, get back on course and get rid of that DEBT! You will be amazed at the feeling you get when you proudly tell the world, or just yourself that you are FINALLY DEBT-FREE!

Essential 6
Every Woman Should Know
How To Negotiate

Women are making more decisions in American households. Their salaries are increasing and they are playing a larger role in making decisions about major purchases. For these reasons, and many others, it's important that women know how to negotiate. For some, the art of negotiating may come easily. For others, it may take some practice. Good negotiating skills will be valuable in day-to-day life and in business. Before you attempt to negotiate anything, make sure you go over this checklist that I created for myself:

- Research, Research, Research! As the saying goes, "Never go into the lion's den unprepared." You should make sure you have investigated multiple sources of information on whatever you are attempting to do to advance yourself. If you want to negotiate your salary, make sure you know what other people in the same position are being paid. If you are purchasing a new vehicle or other major item, make sure you look online and make calls to learn as much as you can about the vehicle you want to purchase.

- Try to keep a positive attitude because you may get denied or rejected. Negativity is not your friend when you are negotiating. If your first offer is turned down, don't get angry because anger can impact the other person's view of you when you return with a counter offer. You need for persons in power to think at least neutrally, if not positively towards you in all negotiations.

- Listen carefully and allow others to speak. The point here is that experts say the majority of people are not good listeners. We are already preparing our response to someone before we hear or understand what the person is saying. You need to listen intently, with an open mind, so that you can go back with an intelligent, thoughtful counter offer. For example, if you are negotiating to buy a car and the car dealership gives you a number of details that go with the purchase, you might offer a counter deal that hurts you because yours excludes what was being offered in the first place. That could be avoided if you listen carefully the first time.

- Unless there is a hard deadline, NEVER feel rushed. If you rush to make a decision, you may end up accepting terms you will soon regret. My own experience that I regretted quickly involved my purchase of an investment property. I thought it was in high demand, so I figured I must offer a high bid, which was accepted. In fact, my information was incorrect and I could have paid a lower price for the property. However, I had signed, and the deal was done! This was a self-imposed rush, and I am happy to say it will never happen again.

- Know your cut-off! In your head or on a sheet of paper, have a list of things that are non-negotiable. You should know your financial "bottom line," after which you will walk away from the deal. You only know this if you've carefully assessed your finances before you approach a major purchase. Typically, we fall in love with a house or a car, which are major purchases. That love could cause us, if we're not careful, to take a "leap of faith" and make the purchase. Later, we realize that we have leaped into a disaster because we never could have afforded the purchase to which we are now obligated. The same could hold true for pursuing that "dream job," only to find that the dream became a nightmare once we signed the contract. All of this could have been avoided if we first knew our cut-off!

- Finally, be ready to walk away. If the other party is not willing to make any concessions, you may have to head for the doors. Many times, you will get a call back. If not, keep on walking and consider another deal. We've all heard the cliché that "when one door closes, another opens."

©Istockphoto.com/shironosov

Whether you recognize it or not, you are negotiating everyday. You negotiate with your spouse, your co-workers, salesmen, and even your kids, depending on the circumstances. The key is for you to become conscious of the many situations in which you are developing your negotiation skills.

Be aware of the times that you are negotiating, and incorporate the best practices that

I have recommended above. Over time, you will get better at it.

Essential 7
Every Woman Should Know
How To Say "NO"

Many women have difficulty saying "No." I would venture to say that it probably doesn't come naturally for most of us. Women tend to be nurturers by nature and are always giving, so the thought of saying "No" may not feel good internally. You may feel like you are going to hurt someone's feelings or let them down. That could be the case, but "No" has to be an answer in certain situations. We have all had different experiences, but here are four common scenarios of when saying "No" is necessary:

(1) When someone asks you to do something that you just do NOT want to do, you should say "No." Because we don't want to make someone feel badly, we agree, but then we feel badly unnecessarily. For example, if asked to join someone shopping, but you know that your budget doesn't allow for that, you must find the word "No" and use it.

(2) When you are making a business decision that may not be beneficial or add value to your business, you should say "No." An example of this would be to consider upgrading your office space. The current setup works for you and your clients, but you want something a little nicer. The reality is that, based on your budget, you should say "No" until you have the finances to comfortably afford the upgrade.

(3) When you get that gut feeling that saying "Yes" will lead to trouble or danger, you must say "No." Women are particularly good at having internal instincts, and we should follow them every time. Consider dating on social media, which is common today. If a woman is offered to meet a stranger in a secluded place, she should say "No," and suggest an alternate, more public place. A money story, though a drastic true-life scenario, is one that I actually heard about. A woman wanted to kill her husband to collect the death benefit from a life insurance policy. She voiced that to someone who offered to take care of her problem and split the money. She didn't say "No," or reconsider the ramifications of doing such a criminal deed, and today she is in jail because of it – without having the death benefit!

(4) When saying "Yes" requires you to put your needs behind someone else's, you must say "No" instead. Let's say you have an important bill to pay, like your mortgage. Someone you love asks to borrow money, and you give it, which causes you to now have insufficient funds for your own bill. That's not only foolish, but it will impact your credit and cause you to incur a late fee. Your needs must come first.

As you can see from the above scenarios, you need to be able to say "No" in your personal life and in business. It may take some practice since saying "No" doesn't come naturally for everyone. Here is how you can do it in three easy steps:

(1) You should forget about being afraid of being rude. Saying "No" is not rude; it *is* an answer. This is especially important for people-pleasers. Notice how many persons you know have little or no trouble telling you "No" without hesitation. Follow their lead and learn from them!

(2) Say "No," just like you would say "Yes." Be firm and confident. For example, you can say "No, not at this time," or "No, unfortunately I can't help you with that," or "No, that doesn't fit into my schedule." Believe me,

you will feel better telling the truth and not trying to please everyone at your expense. Also, people will appreciate you more because they won't automatically assume that your response will always be "Yes."

(3) Always keep in mind that when you say "No" to someone else, you are probably saying "Yes" to YOURSELF, to YOUR family or to YOUR priorities. I'll bet you didn't realize that when you say "Yes" against your will or better judgment, you are shortchanging yourself or the people most dear to you. Your time matters! Say "Yes" to you much more often than you say "Yes" to others.

There you have it, ladies -- and gentlemen. You now have the *Seven Key Essentials* that you need to start your journey towards financial clarity and independence. As you start to incorporate these key essentials into your daily thinking and living, you will start to see a change in your mindset and in your wallet. Your net worth should increase, and your money stresses should decrease. I wish you the best as you start your journey. It's time to make the transition and live your best life!

Reshell Smith, MBA, CFP®

Reshell Smith is a proud mother of one son, CERTIFIED FINANCIAL PLANNER™ professional, Speaker and Author. She is the Founder & President of AMES Financial Solutions, a virtual financial planning firm that she affectionately named after her deceased grandmothers—Ada, Mary, Elizabeth, Sarah. At AMES Financial Solutions, Reshell offers a litany of financial services, from budgeting and investing to end of life planning.

Her greatest passion is promoting financial literacy to children and women. She has educated hundreds of children on how to manage their finances at an early age, so they will make smart money decisions as adults. As well, she hosts and participates in women's empowerment events everywhere. Reshell is an accountability partner for women all over. She *"helps women build wealth, live in abundance and leave a legacy for at least two generations."*

Reshell is available for speaking engagements at women's empowerment workshops, religious institutions, schools, investment conferences, and other events in the financial industry. She is also available for book readings and signings.

Her contact information appears below:

www.reshellsmith.com

info@reshellsmith.com

Made in the USA
Columbia, SC
18 July 2021